ISRAEL AND PALESTINE

Paul Mason

Marshall Cavendish
Benchmark
New York

This edition first published in 2009 in the United States of America by
Marshall Cavendish Benchmark.

Marshall Cavendish Benchmark
99 White Plains Road
Tarrytown, NY 10591
www.marshallcavendish.us

First published in 2008 by
MACMILLAN EDUCATION AUSTRALIA PTY LTD
15–19 Claremont Street, South Yarra 3141

Visit our website at www.macmillan.com.au or go directly to www.macmillanlibrary.com.au

Associated companies and representatives throughout the world.

Copyright © Macmillan Education Australia 2008

Mason, Paul.
    Israel and Palestine / by Paul Mason.
    p. cm. – (Global hotspots)
    Includes index.
    ISBN 978-0-7614-3181-7
    1. Israel–History–Juvenile literature. 2. Palestine–History–Juvenile literature. 3. Arab-Israeli
conflict–Juvenile literature. 4. Arab-Israeli conflict–Occupied territories–Juvenile literature.
5. Arab-Israeli conflict–1993--Peace–Juvenile literature. 6. Israel–Politics and government–
Juvenile literature. 7. Palestinian Arabs–Politics and government–Juvenile literature. I. Title.
DS126.915.M37 2008
956.94–dc22

                                                                    2008018691

MONKEY   Produced for Macmillan Education Australia by
PUZZLE   MONKEY PUZZLE MEDIA LTD
MEDIA   The Rectory, Eyke, Woodbridge, Suffolk IP12 2QW, UK

Edited by Daniel Rogers
Text and cover design by Tom Morris and James Winrow
Page layout by Tom Morris
Photo research by Lynda Lines
Maps by Martin Darlison, Encompass Graphics

Printed in the United States

Acknowledgments
The author and the publisher are grateful to the following for permission to reproduce copyright material:

Front cover photograph: Palestinians wait behind barbed wire at an Israeli army checkpoint to cross into Jerusalem,
October 2007. Courtesy of Getty Images.

Corbis, pp. **12** (Bettmann), **16** (Bettmann), **23** (Peter Turnley), **25** (Peter Turnley); Getty Images, pp. **4** (David Silverman),
6 (After David Roberts), **7** (Brian Hendler), **9** (Hulton Archive), **10** (AFP), **13** (Hulton Archive), **15** (AFP), **17**, **18** (Time & Life
Pictures), **19** (Time & Life Pictures), **20** (AFP), **21** (AFP), **22** (Time & Life Pictures), **23**, **24** (Stephen Ferry), **26** (Marco di Lauro),
27 (AFP), **28** (AFP), **29** (Abid Katib); iStockphoto, p. **30**.

1 3 5 6 4 2

CONTENTS

Glossary words
When a word is printed in **bold**, you can look
up its meaning in the Glossary on page 31.

ALWAYS IN THE NEWS

Global hot spots are places that are always in the news. They are places where there has been conflict between different groups of people for a long time. Sometimes the conflicts have lasted for hundreds of years.

This Palestinian boy is using a sling to hurl stones at Israeli soldiers. He was taking part in an uprising against Israeli control.

Why Do Hot Spots Happen?

There are four main reasons why hot spots happen:

1 Disputes over land, and who has the right to live on it.

2 Disagreements over religion and **culture**, where different peoples find it impossible to live happily side-by-side.

3 Arguments over how the government should be organized.

4 Conflict over resources, such as oil, gold, or diamonds.

Sometimes these disagreements spill over into violence–and into the headlines.

HOT SPOT BRIEFING

NAMES
Israel was **founded** in 1948. For hundreds of years before this, the area was called Palestine.

Israel and Palestine

Israel has been a hot spot since it became a country in 1948. Israel was formed from part of a territory called Palestine. Most Palestinians did not want Israel to be formed. Israelis and Palestinians have been in conflict ever since.

Religion

Israel was founded as a home for people who follow the Jewish religion. Most of the people who came to live there were Jewish. The Palestinians were mainly Muslims. This difference of religion is another cause of conflict between the two peoples.

To the west of the Jewish country of Israel is the Mediterranean Sea. On every other border is a country that is mainly lived in by Arabs and Israelis. There has regularly been violence between Muslim Arabs and Jewish Israelis.

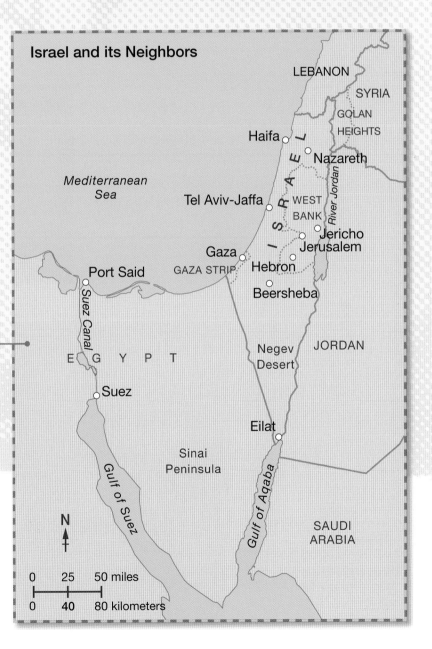

Israel and its Neighbors

ONE LAND, TWO PEOPLES

Among Israelis and Palestinians, there are many who feel that they should be the only ones who live in "their" territory. This is a source of constant disagreement between the two peoples.

Jewish Claims

Many Jews claim that this land is their ancient homeland. Until about 2,000 years ago, it was where most Jewish people lived. Romans ruled the area at the time and the Jews rebelled against them. The Jews were defeated, and many left to live in other places.

HOT SPOT BRIEFING

ZIONISM
In the early 1900s, Jewish people called Zionists began to say that the Jews had a right to return to their ancient home. Some even moved there, in the hope of founding a Jewish settlement that they called Zion.

This painting shows the Jewish rebellion against Roman rule that was quickly stamped out.

Palestinian Claims

The Palestinians also claim that they have an ancient right to live on the land. They were already there more than 1,500 years ago, when Muslim armies conquered the Middle East. This was when many people in the region became Muslims, including most Palestinians. Palestinians have been living in Palestine ever since.

Former Israeli Prime Minister Ariel Sharon visits the Temple Mount in 2000. The visit of a Jewish prime minister to a Muslim holy site (which is also a Jewish holy site) sparked off an uprising by the Palestinians.

FROM THE ROMANS TO WORLD WAR II

After the fall of the **Roman Empire**, one powerful country after another took control of Palestine. By 1516, the **Ottoman Empire** was in command, and it ruled Palestine until 1918.

The Ottoman Empire

The Ottoman Empire was the most powerful empire in the world during the 1500s and 1600s. It stretched across the Middle East, and included parts of Asia, Africa, and Europe. The Ottomans were Muslims, but all religions were allowed under their rule.

End of the Ottoman Empire

The Ottoman Empire ended after World War I. It lost its power and control, so after the war other countries ran many of the Ottoman territories. Britain took control of Palestine.

"No one may prevent them from practicing their [religion] in the churches [or] other places they inhabit."

Sultan Mahmud I, leader of the Ottoman Empire in 1740, confirming that Christian priests were free to preach there. The Jewish religion was also allowed.

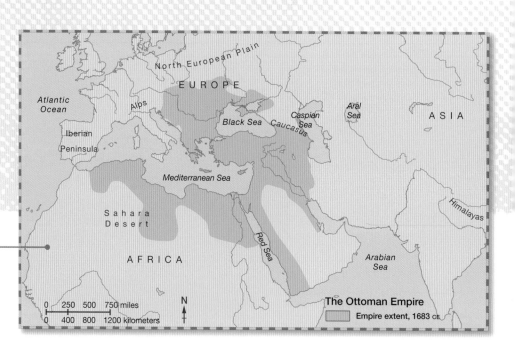

This map shows the area governed by the Ottomans when their empire was at its largest.

Jewish Immigration Increases

The British government allowed Jewish immigrants to settle in Palestine. Throughout the 1920s and 1930s, increasing numbers of Jews arrived. This was unpopular with the Palestinians, who thought of the land as their own. The number of Jews in Palestine increased from about 16 percent in 1914 to 33 percent in 1948.

JEWISH SETTLEMENT

Jewish settlement in Palestine grew rapidly in the 1920s and 1930s.

Populations in Palestine		
	Jews	Palestinians
1914	80,000	500,000
1948	650,000	1,350,000

Rioters in the streets of Jerusalem in 1936. The revolt was led by Palestinians who did not think that the British should be able to force Jewish settlers on them.

THE HOLOCAUST AND THE FOUNDING OF ISRAEL

During World War II (1939–1945) the forces of **Nazi Germany** controlled many areas where Jews lived. The Nazis hated the Jews, and tried to wipe them out. They almost succeeded. Eight million European Jews were deliberately killed by Nazis. This later became known as the Holocaust.

Sympathy for the Jews

Once the war was over, many people wanted to help the Jews who had survived the Holocaust. The world's leaders decided that the Jews should have their own country.

The Founding of Israel

In 1947, the **United Nations** (UN) announced that Palestine would be divided into two areas. One, called Israel, would be Jewish-run. The other, Palestine, would be Arab-run. On May 14, 1948, the new country of Israel was formed.

Celebrating the founding of the state of Israel in 1948.

Arab Resistance

The Palestinian Arabs would not accept the UN plan. They did not want Palestine to be divided, with some of its territory becoming Israel. The Palestinians attacked the Jewish areas, helped by forces from neighboring Arab countries.

Israeli Victory

The Israelis fought back against the Palestinian attacks, and by 1949 had won a big victory. They kept control of Israel, and conquered many of the areas that were to have been Arab-run Palestine as well. Only the west bank of the River Jordan and a strip of land in the south, near Gaza, remained in Palestinian hands.

"Israel has created a new image of the Jew in the world—a picture ... of a people that can fight with heroism."

David Ben Gurion, Israel's first prime minister, after the Jewish victory over Arab forces in 1948–1949.

This map shows how Palestine would have been divided under the terms of the UN partition plan of 1947.

This map shows what actually happened, as Jewish forces took control of large areas the UN intended to be under Arab control.

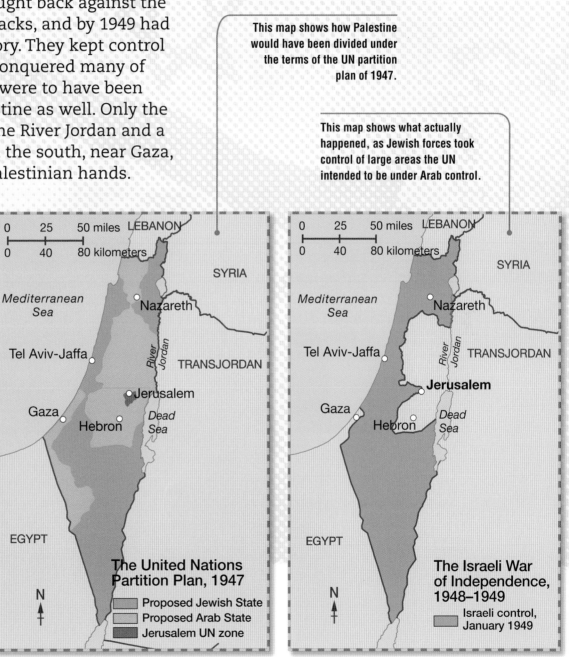

The United Nations Partition Plan, 1947
- Proposed Jewish State
- Proposed Arab State
- Jerusalem UN zone

The Israeli War of Independence, 1948–1949
- Israeli control, January 1949

PALESTINIAN REFUGEES

Almost three-quarters of a million Palestinian **refugees** fled from their homes during the fighting in Israel and Palestine in 1948–1949. Most of these Palestinian refugees left hoping that they would soon return.

The West Bank and the Gaza Strip

The West Bank and the Gaza Strip were the only areas that stayed in Palestinian hands after the fighting. Many Palestinian refugees fled there. In all, about 470,000 people moved to **refugee camps** in the West Bank or the Gaza Strip. These areas soon came under the control of the neighboring Arab countries. Jordan took control of the West Bank, which became part of the Kingdom of Jordan. Egypt controlled the Gaza Strip.

HOT SPOT BRIEFING

ARAB-ISRAELIS
Not all Palestinian Arabs left their homes in 1948–1949. More than 600,000 remained and became Arab-Israeli citizens of the new country, Israel.

Palestinian refugees leave their homes during the fighting of 1948–1949.

Refugee Camps in Other Countries

Some Palestinians left Israel and Palestine altogether, and ended up living in other countries. Most found themselves in refugee camps in Lebanon, Jordan, or Syria. There they began the wait for the chance to return home.

Israel Surrounded

By 1949, Israel was surrounded by **hostile** Arab countries. Many of them now had large populations of Palestinian refugees, who were desperate to return home. Most of the refugees hated the new country of Israel, and wanted to see it destroyed.

Palestinian fighters in the city of Jerusalem, in 1948. Jerusalem was the scene of fierce fighting between Jews and Palestinians.

REFUGEE NUMBERS

STATISTICS

Nearly a quarter of a million Palestinians fled to other countries in 1948–1949:
- 100,000 went to Lebanon
- 75,000 went to Syria
- 70,000 went to Jordan.

ARAB-ISRAELI WARS

From the moment Israel came into existence, it was in conflict with its Arab neighbors. Several times since, the conflict has flared into open war.

1956–Suez

In 1956, Israel claimed it was being threatened by Egypt, and launched an attack. In fact, Israel, Britain, and France had agreed on the attack as a way of getting control of Egypt's Suez Canal. The plan ended up a failure.

1967–The Six-Day War

In 1967, the Egyptian leader General Gamal Abdel Nasser began to say that the Arabs should attack Israel and reclaim the Palestinians' land. On June 5, Israel struck first, attacking Egypt. Syria and Jordan joined on Egypt's side, and the fighting lasted only six days. On June 10, the war ended in a huge victory for Israel. It captured land from Egypt, Syria, and Jordan.

Territory captured by Israel in 1967. The Golan Heights, West Bank, and the Gaza Strip later became known as the "Occupied Territories."

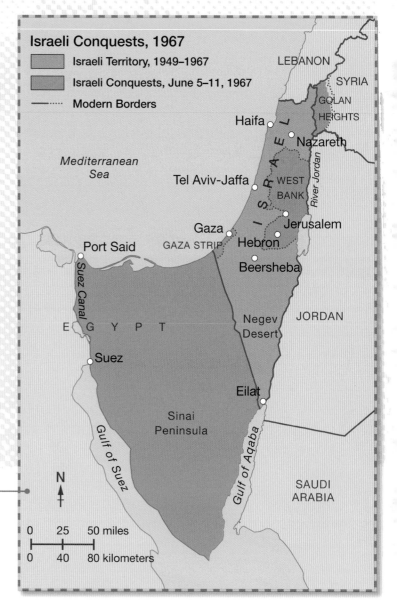

Israeli Conquests, 1967

- Israeli Territory, 1949–1967
- Israeli Conquests, June 5–11, 1967
- ------ Modern Borders

LEBANON
SYRIA
GOLAN HEIGHTS
Haifa
Nazareth
Mediterranean Sea
Tel Aviv-Jaffa
ISRAEL
WEST BANK
River Jordan
Gaza
Jerusalem
GAZA STRIP
Hebron
Port Said
Beersheba
Suez Canal
EGYPT
Negev Desert
JORDAN
Suez
Eilat
Sinai Peninsula
Gulf of Suez
Gulf of Aqaba
SAUDI ARABIA

N

0 25 50 miles
0 40 80 kilometers

1973–The Yom Kippur War

In 1973, Egypt launched a surprise attack on Israel, on the Jewish holiday of Yom Kippur. The Egyptians were still feeling humiliated by their 1967 defeat. They recaptured part of the Sinai Peninsula, but the Israeli general Ariel Sharon led a **counterattack**. The Egyptians were driven back, and the war ended in a **stalemate**.

Camp David

In 1978, Egypt and Israel came together for peace talks at Camp David in the United States. Israel agreed to return the Sinai Peninsula to Egypt. The peace deal was signed in 1979. It officially ended the state of war that had existed between Israel and Egypt since 1948.

The other Arab countries and the Palestinians were furious. They still thought that Israel should not exist. Egypt was alone among its Arab neighbors.

HOT SPOT BRIEFING

THE UNITED NATIONS (UN)
In 1967, the UN called for Israel to leave the territory it had captured in the Six-Day War, in exchange for peace with its Arab neighbors. The UN did not think Israel had the right to control this territory, but Israel ignored the UN's request.

Israeli tanks patrol East Jerusalem, an area they captured from the Palestinians in 1967.

THE GROWTH OF TERRORISM

During the 1967 Six-Day War, the refugee camps in the West Bank and Gaza were captured by Israel. Palestinians who had fled there in 1949 found themselves under Israeli control. A Palestinian named Yasser Arafat began to lead the resistance to Israel.

Palestine Liberation Organization

The 1967 war made many Palestinians feel that they had to rely on themselves to defeat Israel. They could not count on the armies of neighboring Arab countries, which had been crushed by the Israeli forces. An organization called the Palestine Liberation Organization (PLO) led the Palestinian campaign against Israel. The PLO aimed to reclaim Palestine and abolish Israel.

"Today, I have come bearing an olive branch and a freedom fighter's gun. Do not let the olive branch fall from my hand."

PLO leader Yasser Arafat, speaking at the United Nations in 1974. Arafat was hoping that the UN would help the Palestinians against Israel.

Palestinian Liberation Organization leader Yasser Arafat addresses the UN in 1974.

The Palestinian Terror Campaign

The Palestinians had no army to fight the Israelis with, so their most **radical leaders** began a **terrorist** campaign. They hoped that terrorist tactics would force other countries to stop supporting Israel. Palestinian terrorists hijacked aircraft and attacked Israeli targets. They killed Israeli athletes at the Munich Olympics, and murdered passengers on planes.

HOT SPOT BRIEFING

THE MUNICH OLYMPICS
In September 1972, eight members of a Palestinian terrorist group called Black September took prisoner a group of eleven Israeli athletes at the Munich Olympics. Within a short time the Israelis were dead, as were five of the terrorists and a policeman.

A Palestinian terrorist at the 1972 Munich Olympics. Behind the balcony is an apartment where a group of Israeli athletes were held hostage.

THE JEWISH SETTLEMENTS

During the 1980s, the Israeli government encouraged large numbers of Jewish settlers to move from Israel into Palestinian areas. The villages they built were called "settlements."

Why Were the Settlements Built?

The settlements were built because the Israelis wanted to show that the land belonged to them. The land would have been Palestinian under the UN's 1947 plan to divide Palestine, but the plan had never been put into action. Instead, Israeli forces had captured most Palestinian areas. If these areas were filled with Jewish settlers, they might one day become part of Israel, instead of Palestine.

Who Were the Settlers?

Many of the settlers were members of a Jewish religious group called Gush Emunim. They thought it was their duty to build homes in what they saw as their Biblical homeland. Other settlers moved because the land and houses were cheaper than elsewhere in Israel.

Jewish settlements being built in East Jerusalem in 1988. From the 1980s onward, many settlements were built in parts of Palestine where Jews had not previously lived.

Palestinian Objections

The Palestinians objected to the new settlements, because they thought the land belonged to them. They hoped one day to regain control of the 1947 plan's Palestinian areas, and did not want them filled with Jewish settlers. The Palestinians argued that the Israelis were occupying land that did not belong to them.

Water

The Middle East is a dry region, and water is precious. As its settlements expanded into the West Bank, Israel also took control of the main water sources, including the Yarkon-Tanninim aquifer. This underground water store supplies both Jerusalem and Tel Aviv. As a result, some Palestinian farmers began to find it increasingly difficult to water their crops.

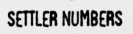

SETTLER NUMBERS

STATISTICS

By 2005, nearly half a million Jewish settlers had moved into Palestinian areas:
- More than 17,000 had moved into the Golan Heights
- Almost 240,000 lived in the West Bank
- Nearly 190,000 had moved into East Jerusalem
- About 9,000 were living in the Gaza Strip.

Resistance to the settlements was so strong that many Israeli settlers felt they needed to carry weapons for protection.

INTIFADA

In 1987, the Palestinians began their first intifada, or rebellion, against the Israeli government.

The First Intifada

The intifada started in December 1987, and the Palestinian protests took several forms:

- Palestinians who worked for Israeli businesses went on strike. The Israelis relied on Palestinian workers, and many businesses suddenly found that they were without most of their employees.
- Protests and demonstrations sprang up in Israel and other countries where Palestinians lived.
- When Israeli troops went into Palestinian areas, the crowds threw stones at them.

The intifada continued until 1993, when it slowly died out.

INTIFADA DEATHS

STATISTICS

By the time the first intifada had ended, it had claimed almost 2,500 lives:
- 1,162 Palestinians had been killed, including 241 children
- 160 Israelis had been killed, five of them children
- Roughly 1,000 Palestinians had been killed by other Palestinians as collaborators (people who were helping the enemy).

Between 1987 and 1991, nightly news clips showed young Palestinians throwing stones at Israeli tanks, or being shot at by soldiers.

Public Opinion Shifts

The intifada changed the way that people outside Israel thought about the Palestinians. Up until then, many people had associated them with terrorism. Now, as in any unequal fight, some people began to side with the underdog. However, when Yasser Arafat declared a Palestinian state in 1988, few world leaders were willing to recognize that it existed.

The Al-Aqsa Intifada

A second major intifada began in 2000, after a visit by the Jewish prime minister Ariel Sharon to Temple Mount. Muslim Palestinians felt that Sharon had shown disrespect for the Al-Aqsa Mosque there, and the angry protests led to a second intifada.

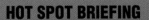

HOT SPOT BRIEFING

THE MUSLIM WORLD
The treatment of Palestinian Muslims during the intifada caused anger among Muslims around the world. They directed their anger mainly at Israel and at the United States, which they saw as Israel's main supporter.

A Palestinian woman shouts at Israeli soldiers. They are guarding a bulldozer that is destroying her home.

THE EMERGENCE OF HAMAS

During the 1990s a rival to the Palestine Liberation Organization sprang up. The new organization was called Hamas, and it quickly began to build support among Palestinians.

The Founding of Hamas

Hamas had been founded in 1987, as the intifada spread through Palestinian communities. It called for the destruction of Israel. Hamas wanted to create a new country that would be run according to the rules of the Muslim religion. It began a terrorist campaign against Israel.

"Observe the popular mood among Palestinians. If people do not want resistance, there will be no resistance."

Khaled Mashaal, Hamas chairman, in Damascus, Syria, April 2005.

The aftermath of a Hamas suicide bomb attack on a bus. Hamas's suicide bombers have included a number of women, among them a mother of five and a mother of two children under the age of ten.

Hamas Tactics

Hamas argued that both soldiers and civilians are acceptable targets. Many of those it has killed have been civilians. Hamas began to attack Israeli targets in several different ways:

- Suicide bombers have strapped explosives to their bodies, gone to public places and blown themselves up. Hamas deliberately chooses crowded places as the sites of its suicide bomb attacks. Buses, restaurants, and supermarkets have all been targeted.

- Since 2002, Hamas has regularly launched rocket attacks on Israeli towns in the Negev region and from across the border in Lebanon.

- Hamas fighters attack the Israeli Army when it enters Palestinian areas, particularly in the Gaza Strip.

Members of Hamas march to celebrate the anniversary of the start of their movement. They are wearing face masks so that the Israeli security forces will not be able to identify them.

OSLO AND THE PALESTINIAN AUTHORITY

During the 1990s, leaders on both the Israeli and Palestinian sides tried to find peaceful solutions to their problems. Their attempts eventually led to a Palestinian Authority, or government, being set up.

Talks in Oslo

From 1992 to 1993, top-secret talks between Israelis and Palestinians were held in Oslo, the capital of Norway. The talks happened because the official peace talks going on elsewhere had achieved nothing. The Oslo talks eventually led to an agreement that the two sides hoped could mean peace.

The Oslo Agreement

The Oslo agreement gave the Palestinians more control over areas where they lived. In return, they were expected to keep the peace. From the start this proved almost impossible. Hamas and other Muslim organizations rejected the Oslo agreement, and began to use suicide bombing to attack Israel.

A famous handshake. Israeli Prime Minister Yitzak Rabin (left) and PLO leader Yasser Arafat shake hands in front of U.S. President Bill Clinton. Rabin was later assassinated by a Jewish extremist.

The Palestinian Authority

The Palestinian Authority eventually gained control over areas in Jericho, the Gaza Strip, and the West Bank:

• In the West Bank, Israel withdrew from places where Palestinians lived, but kept control of areas where there were settlements. Israel also kept control of some territory for what it called "security reasons."

• In the Gaza Strip, many Israeli settlements remained. In 2005, Israel agreed that the settlements there would be abandoned. This left the area completely under Palestinian Authority control. Many settlers refused to leave, and had to be dragged from their homes by Israeli soldiers.

Israelis gather at the Western Wall in Jerusalem to protest against the Oslo agreement.

THE WEST BANK BARRIER

In 2002, Israel began to build a barrier around the West Bank. When finished, the barrier was to be 416 miles (670 kilometers) long. The barrier is the cause of arguments between the Israelis and Palestinians.

What Is the Barrier?

The barrier is part wall and part fence. Most of it is a wire-mesh fence towering more than 16 feet (5 meters) high. To one side is a 13-foot (4-meter) deep ditch and rolls of razor-sharp wire. The barrier has electronic sensors on and around it that can tell if anyone goes near. In some places the barrier is made of more than 26-foot (8-meter) tall concrete blocks instead of wire mesh. Checkpoints in the barrier allow people to pass through.

HOT SPOT BRIEFING

THE BARRIER
The Israelis call the West Bank barrier a "security fence." The Palestinians call it the "apartheid wall."

Graffiti painted on the barrier by the British artist known as Banksy. An old Palestinian man told Banksy the painting made the wall look beautiful. Banksy thanked him, but was told: "We don't want it to be beautiful, we hate this wall. Go home."

Why Was the Barrier Built?

Israelis and Palestinians give different reasons for the building of the barrier:

- The Israeli government says that the barrier is the only way to keep its citizens safe from terrorist attacks.

- The Palestinians say that the barrier is a way of separating them from some of their land. The Israeli side of the barrier includes territory that was intended to be kept by the Palestinians under the 1947 plans.

Palestinians line up to try to get through the barrier. Palestinians whose farms or businesses are on the other side of the wall from their homes have lost their livelihoods.

PROSPECTS FOR PEACE

In 2004, the Palestinian leader Yasser Arafat died. The Israeli government had been against Arafat. With him out of the way, the government was more willing to deal with the Palestinians.

Withdrawal from Gaza

After Arafat's death, the Israeli government withdrew its forces from some of the areas they had first occupied in 1949. In 2005, Jewish settlers left the Gaza Strip. Control of Gaza was handed to the Palestinian Authority. It seemed that perhaps there was some hope that the two sides were finding a way forward.

"The Holy Land is being turned into a wasteland. If an Israeli child is killed and the next day a Palestinian child is killed, it's no solution."

Statement by an Israeli couple whose 14-year-old daughter was killed in a suicide bomb attack.

Paletinians and Israelis gather at the barrier between Jerusalem and the West Bank to demonstrate for peace.

2006–Palestinian Authority Elections

In 2006, elections for the Palestinian Authority took place. The results shocked the world. Arafat's former party, Fatah, lost the election to Hamas. Fatah refused to give up control, and street battles started between the two sides. Hamas forced its way to power in the Gaza Strip, but Fatah kept control of the West Bank.

Impact of the Hamas Victory

After Hamas's election victory it seemed unlikely that progress toward peace could be made. The Israeli government was not willing to deal with an organization that had sent suicide bombers into Israel and killed many Israelis. However, at talks held in Annapolis, Maryland, in 2007, the Israelis and Fatah continued to negotiate. Both hoped that one day an agreement could be reached.

OBSTACLES TO PEACE

Many obstacles to peace remain:

- Deciding on the borders between Israel and Palestine. The 1947 UN borders will now never be put in place, but how close to them will the final borders between Israel and Palestine be?
- The future of the Israeli settlements, in particular the settlements in the West Bank.
- Whether Palestinian refugees can return to places they owned before 1949.
- Israel's security against terrorist attacks, including whether the West Bank barrier should be finished and who should control it.

Fatah supporters run during clashes with the Hamas-controlled police force following Hamas's victory in the election of 2006.

FACTFINDER

ISRAEL

Capital Jerusalem

Area 8,020 square miles
(20,770 square kilometers)

Population 6,276,883

Rate of population change +1.2% per year

Life expectancy 79.6 years

Religions Jewish 80%

Muslim 15%

Christian 2%

Other 3%

Main exports Machinery, software, diamonds, agricultural products, chemicals, textiles

Gross Domestic Product per person*
$20,800

THE WEST BANK

Capital Palestinian Authority HQ is in Ramallah

Area 2,260 square miles (5,860 sq km)

Population 2,385,615

Rate of population change +3.2% per year

Life expectancy 73.5 years

Religions Jewish (in settlements) 17%

Muslim 75%

Christian 8%

Main exports Olives, fruit, vegetables, limestone

Gross Domestic Product per person* $800

THE GAZA STRIP

Capital Gaza City

Area 140 square miles (360 square kilometers)

Population 1,376,289

Rate of population change +3.7% per year

Life expectancy 72.2 years

Religions Jewish 0.6%**

Muslim 98.7%

Christian 0.7%

(**in 2005, before settlements were abandoned)

Main exports Citrus fruit, flowers, textiles

Gross Domestic Product per person* $600

* Gross Domestic Product is the total value of all the goods and services produced by a country in a year divided by the number of people in the country.
(Source for statistics: *CIA World Factbook,* 2008)

The flag of Israel. The West Bank and the Gaza Strip do not have flags of their own.

GLOSSARY

absentee person who is not present

apartheid a policy or practice of separating different races or cultures from one another

counterattack an attack made in response to a first attack from an enemy

culture things that make a group of people distinctive, such as their language, clothes, food, music, songs and stories

founded begun

hostile aggressive toward or strongly opposed to

Middle East region stretching from northeast Africa to southwestern Asia and southeastern Europe, usually said to include Bahrain, Cyprus, Egypt, Iran, Iraq, Israel, Jordan, Kuwait, Lebanon, Oman, Qatar, Saudi Arabia, Sudan, Syria, Turkey, United Arab Emirates, and Yemen

Nazi Germany Germany when the Nazi Party was in charge of the government, between 1933 and 1945

Ottoman Empire large territory controlled by rulers in Istanbul, made up of much of the Middle East and other territories as well

pilgrims religious travelers journeying to a holy site

radical leaders leaders who were willing to use the most extreme tactics

refugee camps places where people who have been forced to leave their homes go to live

Roman Empire large territory controlled by rulers in Rome, made up of southern and western Europe, most of the Middle East, and parts of northern Africa

stalemate a situation where no more progress can be made

terrorist person or people using violence to scare others

United Nations organization set up after World War II that aims to help countries end disputes without fighting

INDEX